THE MOVIE MYSTERY

SUSAN SAUNDERS

ILLUSTRATED BY
THOMAS SPERLING AND SARA KURTZ

A Packard/Montgomery Book

A BANTAM SKYLARK BOOK®
TORONTO • NEW YORK • LONDON • SYDNEY • AUCKLAND

RL 2, 007-009

THE MOVIE MYSTERY
A Bantam Skylark Book / June 1987

CHOOSE YOUR OWN ADVENTURE® is a registered trademark of Bantam Books, Inc.

Original conception of Edward Packard.

*Skylark Books is a registered trademark of Bantam Books, Inc.
Registered in U.S. Patent and Trademark Office and elsewhere.*

ISBN 0-553-15509-1

Published simultaneously in the United States and Canada

*Bantam Books are published by Bantam Books, Inc. Its trade-
mark, consisting of the words "Bantam Books" and the por-
trayal of a rooster, is Registered in U.S. Patent and Trademark
Office and in other countries. Marca Registrada. Bantam
Books, Inc., 666 Fifth Avenue, New York, New York 10103.*

PRINTED IN THE UNITED STATES OF AMERICA

CW   0 9 8 7 6 5 4 3 2 1

"I DON'T LIKE CHOOSE YOUR OWN ADVENTURE® BOOKS. I *LOVE* THEM!" says Jessica Gordon, age ten. And now kids between the ages of six and nine can choose their own adventures too. Here's what kids have to say about the Skylark Choose Your Own Adventure® books.

"These are my favorite books because you can pick whatever choice you want— and the story is all about you."
—**Katy Alson**, *age 8*

"I love finding out how my story will end."
—**Joss Williams**, *age 9*

"I like all the illustrations!"
—**Savitri Brightfield**, *age 7*

"A six-year-old friend and I have lots of fun making the decisions together!"
—**Peggy Marcus** *(adult)*

Bantam Skylark Books in the Choose Your Own Adventure®
Series
Ask your bookseller for the books you have missed

THE
MOVIE
MYSTERY

READ THIS FIRST!!!

Most books are about other people.

This book is about you!

What happens to you depends on what you decide to do.

Do not read this book from the first page through to the last page. Instead, start at page one and read until you come to your first choice. Then turn to the page shown and see what happens.

When you come to the end of a story, go back and try another choice. Every choice leads to a new adventure.

Are you ready to solve the movie mystery? Then turn to page one. LIGHTS! . . . CAMERA! . . . ACTION! . . . and GOOD LUCK!

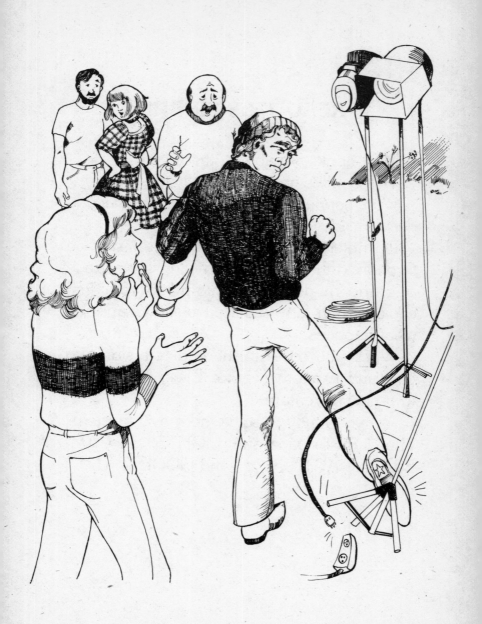

It's summer vacation, and you're visiting **1** your aunt Molly on location in the Canadian woods. "On location" is movie talk for a place outside the studio where a film is being made.

Aunt Molly is a stunt woman. Right now she's working as a double for one of the young movie stars. Her trick dog Sam is in the film, too, along with a trained bear named Percy.

There's trouble just after you arrive. The director has to fire a couple of the local crew members. One of them is a man named Red Larkin. As he leaves the set, Larkin kicks over some movie lights with his cowboy boots. It looks like an accident, but you think he did it on purpose.

After that, things go well. The movie should be finished on time. Aunt Molly and Sam are making lots of money. And you're having fun learning some of the easy stunts.

Turn to page 2.

2   In the scene being filmed next, the young star is chased by a bear. She gets away by jumping off a cliff into the river.

Wearing a blond wig, Aunt Molly will jump off the cliff into a hidden safety net. Then the young actress will make a short jump into the water. When the two pieces of film are put together, it will look as though the girl made a daredevil leap.

It's a simple stunt. But when Aunt Molly jumps, part of the net pulls loose—and she sprains her shoulder. She says she's fine, but she groans when the director says he wants to film the jump again.

Just then a crewman runs up. "Sam has disappeared from your trailer!" he tells Aunt Molly.

"Oh, no," she says. "He's in the next scene." She turns to you. "Will you try to find him while I do the stunt again?"

Should you look for Sam? Or should you ask Aunt Molly if you can do the stunt for her?

Go on to the next page.

If you offer to take Aunt Molly's place,
turn to page 8.

If you decide to look for Sam,
turn to page 10.

Aunt Molly, the movie director, and three of the crewmen go with you to the trailer. You show them the prints leading into the trees.

"There's no proof that those are from Red's boots," says the director. "Or that they'll lead us to Sam."

"But they're the only clue we have," says Aunt Molly. "Let's see where they go."

You follow the others into the woods. It's getting dark. One of the men has brought along a flashlight. Still, it's hard to see the trail. When you're deep in the forest, you think you hear a noise.

"Aunt Molly," you whisper.

"Shhh!" she warns. "We don't want the dognapper to know we're after him."

You *did* hear something. It could have been the wind—but what if it was Red? Should you go find out? Or should you stay with the group?

If you stay with the others, turn to page 33.

If you decide to find out what made the noise, turn to page 34.

That bear weighs around 400 pounds. Even if he just steps on you, it will be pretty serious.

"Jump!" the director shouts.

So you jump. As you hit the net, you hear a ripping sound. Oh, no! The ropes holding the net have broken!

You're wrapped in the net like potatoes in a bag, hanging over the river. One rope is still holding . . . but for how long?

There's a bush not too far away. Should you try to swing and grab it? Or should you move as little as possible and hope someone reaches you before you drop forty feet?

If you stay still and wait for help,
turn to page 13.

If you try to grab the bush, turn to page 38.

8   At first Aunt Molly doesn't want you to do the stunt.

"But I've jumped into a net lots of times," you remind her. "It's the first thing you taught me to do."

"Let the kid try it once," says the director. "Rest your shoulder for a while."

Finally Aunt Molly says okay. You're worried about Sam. But you're excited that you're going to be in the movie!

The dress Aunt Molly wears for the scene has to be shortened, although she isn't much taller than you are. You put it on, along with the blond wig. Then you walk to the edge of the cliff and look down at the river, almost forty feet below. The large safety net is much closer —only seven or eight feet below.

A crewman checks the net to make sure the corners are tied tight. Then the director explains the scene.

Turn to page 26.

10   You think Aunt Molly is more worried about Sam than about doing the stunt with a hurt shoulder. "I'll find Sam," you tell her.

First you go to Aunt Molly's trailer, just to see if Sam has come back. He isn't there. But near the door you spot something. It's a very clear print of a cowboy boot, with a star cut into the heel. Who could have made it? Most of the movie crew wear sneakers.

You find a second print at the edge of the woods. Then you see a third a little beyond that. The person who made those prints might know where Sam is. Or maybe he took Sam away!

You could wait until Aunt Molly's scene is finished and then show her what you've found. But by then Sam might be miles away. Or you could follow the prints right now, even though you're not supposed to go into the woods alone.

If you follow the prints into the woods, turn to page 16.

If you go back to get Aunt Molly, turn to page 20.

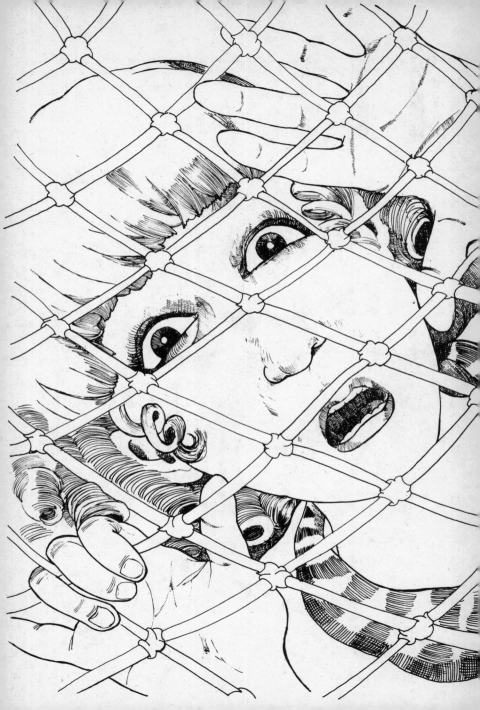

The last rope is about to give way. You can only hope it will hold until someone gets to you.

"Help!" you yell.

You can hear Aunt Molly above you: "Try not to move. We're coming down."

You hear the tearing sound again. Now a man is coming toward you along the cliff side. It's Red Larkin! Could he be the person you saw near the net before you jumped? Even if he wants to help you, he's too far away.

Rrriiipp! The rope pulls apart, and you drop like a stone toward the river. How can you swim wrapped in a net? This is it, you think. . . .

Turn to page 41.

You start to step into the canoe.

"Hold it," Red Larkin says. He pulls a rubber plug out of his pocket. Then he jams it into a hole in the bottom of the canoe. "I figured this would keep nosy visitors away from the island." He laughs. "Now get in."

You climb into the bow. Then he pushes the canoe into the water and starts to paddle across the lake.

Red thinks he's pretty smart to have drilled that hole. But you're pretty smart, too. And that plug has given you an idea. Just before you reach the island, you work it out of the hole with your foot. You lean forward, pretending to scratch your ankle. Then you pick up the plug and stick it in your pocket.

"We'll see who has the last laugh!" you think.

Turn to page 44.

16   You've promised Aunt Molly that you'll never go into the woods by yourself. But this is an emergency! Here's another print, near this path. And aren't these dog tracks next to it?

The path winds through the pines. You follow it to the shore of a lake. At the edge of the water you find the boot prints again. And, clearly this time, you see the prints of a large dog. The person wearing the cowboy boots dognapped Sam! You're sure of that now.

A rocky island rises out of the lake. Could Sam be there? You don't think you can swim that far. But you find an old canoe dragged into the trees. It's in pretty bad shape. Still, it might get you to the island and back.

Should you try it? Or should you call Sam's name from the shore? If he hears you, he'll bark. That way you'll know he's on the island. But the dognapper may hear you, too.

If you decide to try the canoe,
turn to page 18.

If you decide to call Sam, turn to page 22.

18   You pull the canoe down to the lake and climb in. You haven't paddled far when you hear a nasty laugh behind you. A man is standing on shore, watching you. It's Red Larkin. You remember he kicked over the lights the day he was fired from the movie crew. And you remember something else. He was wearing cowboy boots!

All too soon you know why he's laughing. The canoe is filling up with water. A neat round hole has been drilled into the bottom. You pull off your shoe and sock and stuff the end of your sock into the hole. But it doesn't do much good.

"You may make it over to the island to join **19** that dog," Red shouts. "But you won't make it back." He laughs again. Then he disappears into the woods.

The wind picks up. The water is getting rougher and rougher. And you're still some way from the island when the canoe slowly sinks into the lake.

Turn to page 47.

20   Aunt Molly will know what to do. You hurry back to the cliff edge. But they aren't shooting the scene. They discovered that some of the ropes holding the safety net had been cut. And now they're wondering if it was an accident that the ropes gave way the first time Aunt Molly did the jump.

"I couldn't find Sam," you tell them. "But I did find some prints near the trailer. Cowboy boots—with stars on the heels." Just as you say it, you remember something: Red Larkin was wearing cowboy boots when he kicked over the movie lights.

"Red Larkin," you say out loud.

"That's right," says Aunt Molly. "He always wore fancy cowboy boots. But he left a long time ago."

"Or at least we thought he did," says the director. "Show us those prints!"

Turn to page 4.

22   "Sam!" you shout. You hear an answering bark. Sam's on the island, all right. But you don't see him. Then you hear him whining, and you realize he must be tied up.

You're about to push the old canoe into the water when someone grabs you from behind. It's Red Larkin! And then you remember: Red was wearing cowboy boots the day he was fired!

"I'll make them sorry," Red brags. "Now I've got you *and* the dog. And they'll be having a little more trouble with the safety net, too."

So Red was the one behind Aunt Molly's accident!

He shoves you toward the canoe. Should you try to get away? Or would that be too risky? Red is a lot bigger than you. And from the way he grabbed you, you know he's strong.

---

*If you think you'd better go with Red,
turn to page 15.*

*If you decide you'll try to escape,
turn to page 29.*

24   You think you'll have a better chance with a trained bear than with a net that might drop you forty feet into the river.

You read a story once about a wild bear walking into someone's tent in the woods. The thing to do, the story said, is play dead. So you close your eyes and fall to the ground.

"Cut!" the director yells. "Has the kid fainted?"

"It's probably stage fright," says one of the cameramen.

You feel the bear's hot breath on your cheek. You wait for his sharp teeth to close on your nose. . . .

A big, wet tongue licks your face.

"Percy!" Aunt Molly shouts. "Stop that!"

Turn to page 31.

"Look behind you, then start running, as though something has frightened you," the director tells you. "When you get to that tree, we'll turn Percy loose. Stop for a second on the edge of the cliff . . . then jump!"

You're ready. "Action!" the director shouts.

You run to the edge of the cliff and get set to jump. . . . Wait! There's someone down there. Is he doing something to the net?

But here comes the bear. Is Percy smiling
. . . or growling? He's supposed to be tame,
but he looks plenty fierce.

Should you jump? What if the net pulls loose
again? You could fall forty feet. On the other
hand, what will the bear do if he catches up
with you?

If you decide to jump, turn to page 7.

*If you decide you'd rather face the bear,
turn to page 24.*

You pretend to stumble and fall. Before Red **29** can grab you, you scramble forward into the trees. You run as fast as you can. Finally you realize that you've escaped from Red—and lost the trail.

It's getting dark when you see the bear. "It's Percy," you think. He probably got loose and went for a walk. Now he's on his way back to the movie camp for dinner. You can follow him home.

The bear jogs through the woods as though he's in a hurry. You're getting tired. "Percy, slow down!" you shout.

The bear turns around. . . . *It's not Percy!* It stands up on its hind legs and growls at you.

If this were a movie, what would Aunt Molly do? Too bad this is real life—and that's a real bear!

"AUNT MOLLY, RED LARKIN, ANY-BODY . . . H-E-E-E-L-L-L-P!"

The End

"Are you okay?" Aunt Molly sounds worried.

"I'm all right," you tell her, opening your eyes. "But I saw someone on the cliff side. He could have been fooling around with the safety net."

"I don't see anyone now," says the director. "But if you're worried, we'll check the net again and take a look around."

Two of the crewmen start to climb down the cliff. "Could you come along and show us where you saw the guy?" one of them asks you.

"Better not." The director shakes his head. "You look kind of pale." And when you stand up, you do feel a little dizzy.

If you decide to stay on top of the cliff, turn to page 43.

If you say, "I'll climb down," turn to page 36.

You might get lost if you left the others now. **33**
Besides, the noise was probably just the wind.

The trail takes you to the edge of a lake.
"Listen," Aunt Molly says. "That's Sam's
bark—I'd know it anywhere! He's on that
island."

The others go back to get a rubber raft. But
Aunt Molly says, "Sam hates to be outside by
himself at night." So you and she keep him
company by singing at the top of your lungs
until the men get back.

Then you row across the lake to the island.
There's no one in sight. But there are star-
heeled boot prints all around the tree where
Sam is chained. He is worn out but safe and
sound.

"Obviously, Red Larkin—or whoever it
was—did his mischief and sneaked away," says
Aunt Molly. "I doubt if he'll be back."

"Maybe not," you say. "But I'd feel a whole
lot better if we had solved this mystery."

The End

You creep through the darkness, listening hard. Someone grabs your arm! It's Red Larkin! You jerk away and start running through the dark woods. But he follows. Suddenly you find yourself hurtling down a hill.

You know what to do—you've seen Aunt Molly do it many times. You cover your head with your arms, bend your knees, and double up into a loose ball. You roll to the bottom bruised but okay.

But Red doesn't know anything about stunts. Halfway down the hill, he hits his head on a tree stump and knocks himself out.

Aunt Molly calls, "Where are you?"

"Down here," you shout. "And I've got Red!"

"Great work!" the director says, coming up with the crewmen. "You're a regular stunt kid."

"And a pretty good detective, too," Aunt Molly adds. "You've solved the movie mystery."

The End

36 You won't be climbing down very far. But Aunt Molly insists on tying a rope around your waist. Then she holds the other end while you go over the edge of the cliff like a mountain climber.

You look around. Right near the net you find a boot print with a star in the heel. Then you have uninvited company. Percy has decided that he likes you and has scrambled down the cliff behind you.

He sniffs the air for a minute. Has he found a clue? He rushes past you, gets tangled in your rope, and drags you along after him.

Suddenly he slips! The end of the rope is jerked out of Aunt Molly's hands, and you and Percy are faaaaaalling. . . .

As you fly through the air toward the river, you have one thought: "I hope a 400-pound bear floats!"

The End

You get the net swinging toward the bush. And somehow you manage to grab it—just before the last rope breaks. But your troubles are far from over! You're pulling the plant's roots right out of the cliff side.

"Quick—take my hand!" a voice says. It's Red Larkin, that guy who was fired. He pulls you safely to a narrow rock ledge.

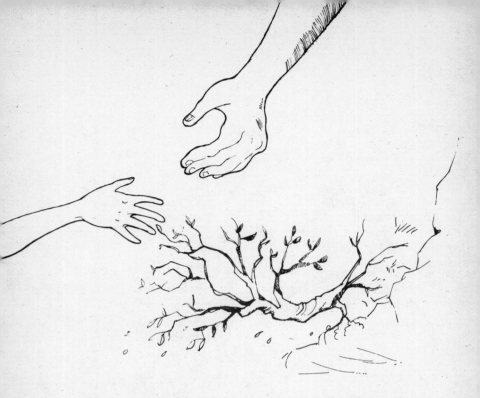

"I wanted to mess up the movie," he mutters. "But not if it means messing up a kid."

When you were standing on top of the cliff, wearing the blond wig and dress, he thought you were your aunt.

"I knew Molly could take care of herself," Red says. "She did the first time I cut the ropes. Besides, I didn't cut *all* of them. I just wanted to scare people—not hurt anyone."

Turn to page 51.

Smack! You fall right onto the rubber raft holding the second cameraman. You bounce into the air and back down onto the raft, knocking the cameraman—and his gear—into the river. But you're safe!

You look up in time to see the director dragging Red Larkin up the cliff. You find out later that Red has been sneaking around the set since he was fired, trying to make trouble for the movie. Twice he cut the ropes holding the net. And he also hid Sam. At the end, though, he did try to help you.

"Pretty good stunt, kid," the director says that evening. "But the light wasn't quite right. I'll let you try it again tomorrow. We'll shoot it from the point when the ropes break."

Luckily, he's only kidding . . . isn't he?

The End

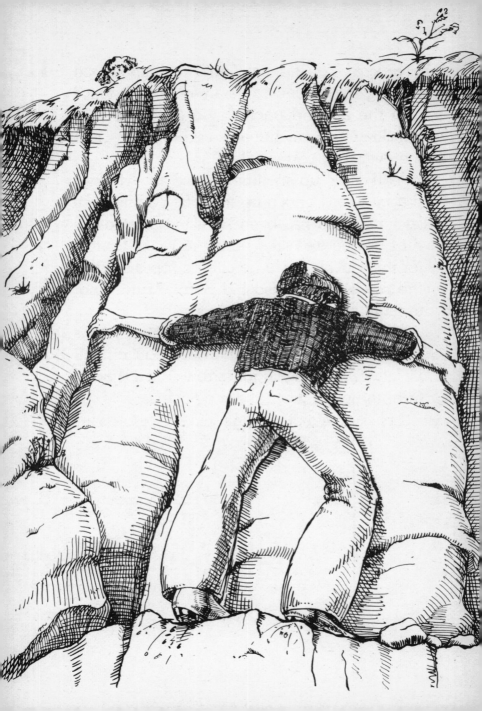

You're feeling shaky from all that bear **43**
breath. So you stay on top of the cliff and watch
the crewmen climb down.

They stop at the net. "Some of the ropes
have been cut!" one of them shouts.

You see something move behind a boulder.
As you watch, a man stands up and starts inch-
ing his way across the cliff face toward some
trees. "There's the guy!" you yell.

"Get him!" shouts the director.

The crewmen scramble across the cliff. But
the sun is setting. It's the time of day when
everything looks gray and brown—like the cliff
itself. And they can't seem to see the mystery
man from where they are.

Everyone on top of the cliff is shouting
directions: "He's over there!" "A little to your
left!" "You're too far down!" And that makes
things worse.

You're afraid the man will get away.

Turn to page 48.

44   Red leads you to the middle of the island. Sam is there, chained to a tree. When he sees you, he barks and wags his tail. But he growls at Red Larkin.

Red ties you to a tree near the dog. "So you won't be lonesome," he says with a mean laugh. "Now I'll go back and see what other trouble I can make."

But you know something he doesn't: You have the plug, and he's not going anywhere. You know something else, too. Sam doesn't usually bite. But when he hears the word *Mayday,* he knows he's supposed to knock a person flat, stand on him, and bite if he has to.

Sam is also good at chewing through rope. Your hands are free almost before Red is out of sight. You unchain the dog, and the two of you sneak into the woods to wait.

Mr. Larkin is going to have a few unpleasant surprises when he comes back.

The End

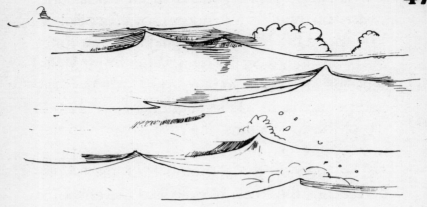

Luckily, you're a strong swimmer, and you can swim the rest of the way to the island. Then what about getting back to shore? Alone, you'd never make it.

But you won't be alone. You'll have Sam— and Sam is a trick dog. You'll get him to do one of his best stunts from the movie: pull a kid, who's holding onto his collar, across a lake to safety. And this time, you'll be playing the kid.

"Sam!" you call. And you hear a welcoming bark.

The End

48   Thinking quickly, you run up a ladder and switch on one of the huge movie spotlights. You move the top of the big light around until the beam shines on the man. When Aunt Molly sees what you're doing, she switches on another spotlight. He's caught right in the middle of the two beams. It's Red Larkin! Somehow you're not surprised.

The men on the cliff grab Red just before he reaches the trees. It looks like the end of a movie, the part where the good guys get the bad guy.

"I'll give you another chance at the jump tomorrow," the director says to you later. "Maybe you'll grow up to be a famous stunt person, like your aunt."

"I think I'd rather be a director," you tell him. "And maybe I won't have to wait until I grow up. I already have a great idea for a movie. It'll be called *The Movie Mystery*. And we have all the actors we need right here."

Except for Red Larkin, of course. You have a feeling he'll be in jail for a while.

The End

Red Larkin is telling the truth. The last rope **51** was cut when it rubbed on the sharp edge of a rock. He *did* cut the other ropes both times. And it turns out he's the one who kidnapped Sam. But he's not all bad.

When you landed in the net, Red saw that you weren't Molly. So he climbed back across the cliff and saved you. And he tells you where to find Sam—safe and sound. So you feel a little sorry for him when the sheriff comes to take him to jail. But the show must go on.

What about the scene you were doing? The director says it can wait for a couple of days, until Aunt Molly's shoulder heals. So it looks as if your career as a movie double is over.

Maybe that's just as well. After your adventure, you've decided that one stunt person in the family is plenty!

The End

ABOUT THE AUTHOR

Susan Saunders grew up on a ranch in Texas, where she learned rodeo riding. A graduate of Barnard College, she has been a ceramicist and an editor of filmstrips for children. She is the author of seven books for young readers, including *Wales' Tale,* a Junior Literary Guild selection; *The Green Slime, The Creature From Miller's Pond, Ice Cave,* and *Runaway Spaceship*—four other titles in the Bantam Skylark Choose Your Own Adventure series.

ABOUT THE ILLUSTRATORS

Thomas Sperling was raised in Florida. He studied fine arts at St. Andrews College in North Carolina, where he received his BFA degree. He currently lives and works in New York City, illustrating for books and magazines.

Sara Kurtz was born in Canada and studied fine arts at the University of Windsor, in Ontario. Now living in New York, she produces filmstrips and illustrates books for children. Her drawings appeared in *Wild Horse Country,* a Bantam Skylark Choose Your Own Adventure.

CHOOSE YOUR OWN ADVENTURE

SKYLARK EDITIONS

☐	15480	The Green Slime #6 S. Saunders	$2.25
☐	15532	Help! You're Shrinking #7 E. Packard	$2.25
☐	15496	Indian Trail #8 R. A. Montgomery	$2.25
☐	15506	Dream Trips #9 E. Packard	$2.25
☐	15495	The Genie In the Bottle #10 J. Razzi	$2.25
☐	15222	The Big Foot Mystery #11 L. Sonberg	$1.95
☐	15424	The Creature From Miller's Pond #12 S. Saunders	$2.25
☐	15226	Jungle Safari #13 E. Packard	$1.95
☐	15442	The Search For Champ #14 S. Gilligan	$2.25
☐	15444	Three Wishes #15 S. Gilligan	$2.25
☐	15465	Dragons! #16 J. Razzi	$2.25
☐	15489	Wild Horse Country #17 L. Sonberg	$2.25
☐	15262	Summer Camp #18 J. Gitenstein	$1.95
☐	15490	The Tower of London #19 S. Saunders	$2.25
☐	15501	Trouble In Space #20 J. Woodcock	$2.25
☐	15283	Mona Is Missing #21 S. Gilligan	$1.95
☐	15418	The Evil Wizard #22 A. Packard	$2.25
☐	15306	The Flying Carpet #25 J. Razzi	$1.95
☐	15318	The Magic Path #26 J. Goodman	$1.95
☐	15467	Ice Cave #27 Saunders/Packard	$2.25
☐	15342	The Fairy Kidnap #29 S. Gilligan	$1.95
☐	15463	Runaway Spaceship #30 S. Saunders	$2.25
☐	15508	Lost Dog! #31 R. A. Montgomery	$2.25
☐	15379	Blizzard of Black Swan #32 Saunders/Packard	$2.25
☐	15380	Haunted Harbor #33 S. Gilligan	$2.25
☐	15399	Attack of the Monster Plants #34 S. Saunders	$2.25

Prices and availability subject to change without notice.

Match Wits with America's
Sherlock Holmes in
Sneakers

ENCYCLOPEDIA BROWN

With a head full of facts and his
eyes and ears on the world of
Idaville, meet Leroy (Encyclo-
pedia) Brown. Each Encyclope-
dia Brown book contains 10 baf-
fling cases to challenge, stymie
and amuse young sleuths. Best
of all, the reader can try solving
each case on his own before
looking up the solution in the
back of the book. "BRIGHT
AND ENTERTAINING. . . ."
The New York Times
By Donald Sobol

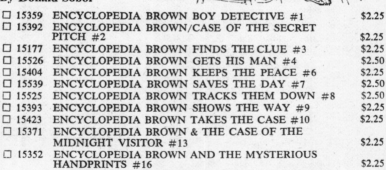